From Idea to Success

Strategies for Building and Scaling a
Thriving Business

John Chairez

Table of contents

INTRODUCTION

Why entrepreneurship is essential for business success

Entrepreneurship is essential for business success because it drives innovation, creates job opportunities, and fosters economic growth. Entrepreneurs are the driving force behind new businesses and new ideas that can change the world. They are the ones who take the risk and bring new products, services, and processes to the market, often disrupting existing industries.

Entrepreneurship is crucial for economic growth because it creates jobs, stimulates innovation, and generates new revenue streams. Entrepreneurs are job creators, and the businesses they start often employ large numbers of people, contributing to the overall economic growth of their communities and countries.

Entrepreneurship also fosters innovation, which is essential for businesses to remain competitive and relevant in the fast-paced, ever-changing world of business. Entrepreneurs are often the ones who identify gaps in the market and create products and services that meet those needs. They are not bound by traditional ways of thinking and are more likely to take risks and experiment with new ideas.

Moreover, entrepreneurship can provide a way for individuals to achieve financial independence and personal fulfillment. Starting a business can be a way to pursue one's passion, achieve greater control over one's work-life balance, and build wealth.

In contrast, businesses that do not embrace entrepreneurship may struggle to remain relevant and competitive. They may become complacent, rely on outdated business models and processes, and may miss out on opportunities for growth and innovation.

In conclusion, entrepreneurship is essential for business success because it drives innovation, creates jobs, fosters economic growth, and enables individuals to pursue their passions and achieve financial independence. Businesses that embrace entrepreneurship are more likely to remain competitive and relevant in the long term, while those that do not may struggle to survive in an increasingly competitive marketplace.

The Benefits and Challenges of Entrepreneurship

Entrepreneurship offers many benefits, including the ability to create one's schedule, pursue one's passion, and potentially build a successful and profitable business. However, entrepreneurship also comes with significant challenges that entrepreneurs must navigate in order to achieve success.

One of the key benefits of entrepreneurship is the ability to create one's own schedule and work on projects that align with one's personal interests and values. This can be particularly appealing for individuals who are dissatisfied with their current jobs or who want greater control over their professional lives. Entrepreneurship also offers the potential to build significant wealth and financial independence, particularly for successful entrepreneurs who are able to scale their businesses and generate significant revenue.

Another benefit of entrepreneurship is the ability to create jobs and positively impact the local economy. Successful entrepreneurs are often able to hire employees and create new opportunities for individuals in their communities. Entrepreneurship can also lead to the development of new products and services that solve important problems and improve people's lives.

However, entrepreneurship also comes with significant challenges that entrepreneurs must navigate in order to achieve success. One of the biggest challenges is the risk involved in starting a new business. Entrepreneurship often requires significant financial investment, and there is no guarantee that the business will be successful. Entrepreneurs must be willing to take on this risk and be prepared to weather the ups and downs of starting a new business.

Another challenge of entrepreneurship is the need to wear many hats. Entrepreneurs are often responsible for a wide range of tasks, including marketing, sales, accounting, and operations. This can be overwhelming and time-consuming, particularly for entrepreneurs who are just starting out.

Entrepreneurship can also be emotionally challenging. Starting a new business can be stressful, and entrepreneurs may face criticism, rejection, and setbacks along the way. It is important for entrepreneurs to develop resilience and perseverance in order to overcome these challenges and stay focused on their goals.

In conclusion, entrepreneurship offers many benefits, including the ability to create one's own schedule, pursue one's passion, and potentially build a successful and profitable business. However, entrepreneurship also comes with significant challenges, including financial risk, the need to wear many hats and emotional challenges. Entrepreneurs who are able to navigate these challenges and stay focused on their goals are more likely to achieve success in the long term.

CHAPTER 1

Developing an Entrepreneurial Mindset

Characteristics of successful entrepreneurs

Successful entrepreneurs share several common characteristics that contribute to their ability to start and grow successful businesses. These characteristics include:

1. Passion and persistence: Successful entrepreneurs are passionate about their business ideas and are willing to put in the hard work and persistence needed to turn those ideas into reality. They are driven by a sense of purpose and are not deterred by setbacks or failures.

2. Creativity and innovation: Successful entrepreneurs are able to think outside the box and come up with new and innovative ideas. They are able to identify problems and opportunities that

others may overlook and are not afraid to take risks in pursuit of their goals.

3. Adaptability: Successful entrepreneurs are able to adapt to changing circumstances and market conditions. They are flexible in their approach and are willing to pivot their strategies as needed to stay competitive and meet the needs of their customers.

4. Strong work ethic: Successful entrepreneurs are hardworking and willing to put in the time and effort needed to succeed. They are able to manage their time effectively and prioritize their tasks in order to maximize their productivity.

5. Resilience: Successful entrepreneurs are able to bounce back from setbacks and failures. They are able to learn from their mistakes and use those experiences to grow and improve their businesses.

6. Leadership: Successful entrepreneurs are able to inspire and motivate others. They are able to build and lead a team of employees who share their vision and are committed to helping the business succeed.

7. Financial acumen: Successful entrepreneurs have a solid understanding of financial principles and are able to manage their finances effectively. They are able to make informed decisions about investments, cash flow, and revenue generation.

In conclusion, successful entrepreneurs possess a combination of passion, creativity, adaptability, strong work ethic, resilience, leadership, and financial acumen. By cultivating these characteristics, aspiring entrepreneurs can increase their chances of success and build businesses that make a positive impact on their communities and the world.

Overcoming limiting beliefs and embracing risk-taking

Limiting beliefs are negative thoughts and attitudes that hold us back from achieving our full potential. These beliefs can be deeply ingrained and can prevent us from taking risks and pursuing our dreams. In order to overcome limiting beliefs and embrace risk-taking, it is important to identify and challenge these beliefs.

One of the first steps in overcoming limiting beliefs is to become aware of them. This can involve taking stock of our thoughts and attitudes and identifying any negative self-talk or patterns of thinking that are holding us back. Once we have identified these beliefs, we can begin to challenge them and replace them with more positive and empowering beliefs.

It can also be helpful to seek out support and guidance from others. This might involve talking to a mentor or coach, joining a support group, or seeking out resources such as books or podcasts that focus on personal development and overcoming limiting beliefs.

Another key to overcoming limiting beliefs is to take small, manageable risks. This can involve trying new things, taking on new challenges, and stepping outside of our comfort zones. By taking these risks, we can build our confidence and develop a sense of resilience that can help us overcome future challenges.

It is also important to embrace failure as a natural part of the learning process. Rather than viewing failure as a sign of weakness or inadequacy, we can reframe it as an opportunity for growth and learning. By embracing failure and viewing it as a necessary step on the path to success, we can become more comfortable with taking risks and pursuing our goals.

In conclusion, overcoming limiting beliefs and embracing risk-taking is essential for personal and professional growth. By becoming aware of our limiting beliefs, seeking out support and guidance, taking small risks, and embracing failure, we can develop the resilience and confidence needed to pursue our dreams and achieve our full potential.

Building a growth-oriented mindset

A growth-oriented mindset is essential for personal and professional development. It involves the belief that our abilities and intelligence can be developed through hard work and dedication, rather than being fixed traits that we are born with. By building a growth-oriented mindset, we can become more resilient, adaptable, and open to learning and new experiences.

Here are some strategies for building a growth-oriented mindset:

1. Embrace challenges: Challenges and obstacles are opportunities for growth and learning. Rather than avoiding them, seek out challenges that will push you outside of your comfort zone and help you develop new skills.

2. View failure as feedback: Failure is not a reflection of our abilities or intelligence, but rather a natural part of the learning process. Instead of giving up when you encounter failure, view it as feedback and an opportunity to learn and improve.

3. Learn from others: Seek out mentors, coaches, and other successful individuals who can provide guidance and support as you work towards your goals. Surround yourself with people who inspire you and who have a growth-oriented mindset.

4. Cultivate a love of learning: Continuously seek out new knowledge and skills. Read books, attend

workshops and seminars, and take courses that align with your goals and interests.

5. Take risks: Taking calculated risks is an essential part of growth and development. Identify opportunities that align with your goals and take action, even if it means stepping outside of your comfort zone.

6. Focus on the process, not just the outcome: Rather than obsessing over the end result, focus on the steps you need to take to get there. Celebrate small wins and milestones along the way, and use setbacks and failures as opportunities for learning and growth.

In conclusion, building a growth-oriented mindset requires a commitment to continuous learning, embracing challenges and failure, seeking out support and guidance, and taking calculated risks. By adopting a growth-oriented mindset, you can develop the resilience and skills needed to achieve your goals and reach your full potential.

CHAPTER 2

Ideation and Innovation

Identifying opportunities for innovation

Identifying opportunities for innovation is crucial for businesses looking to stay competitive and drive growth. However, it can be challenging to identify new opportunities, especially in industries that are constantly evolving. Here are some strategies for identifying opportunities for innovation:

1. Monitor industry trends: Stay up-to-date with the latest trends and technologies in your industry. Attend conferences, read industry publications, and follow thought leaders in your field to stay informed.

2. Gather customer feedback: Talk to your customers and gather feedback about their needs

and pain points. Use this information to identify opportunities for new products or services.

3. Study your competitors: Analyze your competitors' products and services to identify gaps in the market. Look for areas where you can differentiate yourself and offer something new and unique.

4. Leverage new technologies: Keep an eye on emerging technologies that could be applied to your industry. For example, artificial intelligence, blockchain, and virtual reality are all technologies that are transforming industries in unique ways.

5. Analyze internal processes: Look for ways to streamline internal processes and improve efficiency. This could involve implementing new software or tools or rethinking the way certain tasks are completed.

6. Explore new markets: Consider expanding into new markets or offering your products and services to a new audience. This could involve expanding into international markets or targeting a new demographic within your existing market.

7. Collaborate with others: Collaborate with other businesses, universities, or research institutions to identify new opportunities for innovation. This can bring fresh perspectives and expertise to your organization.

In conclusion, identifying opportunities for innovation is essential for driving business growth and staying competitive. By staying informed about industry trends, gathering customer feedback, studying competitors, leveraging new technologies, analyzing internal processes, exploring new markets, and collaborating with others, businesses can identify new opportunities and innovate in unique and meaningful ways.

Developing new products and services

Developing new products and services is an essential part of growing a business and staying competitive. Here are some strategies for developing new products and services:

1. Identify customer needs: Conduct market research and gather feedback from customers to identify their needs and pain points. Use this information to generate ideas for new products or services that address these needs.

2. Brainstorm ideas: Encourage idea-sharing among team members and brainstorm ideas for new products or services. Evaluate each idea based on its potential to meet customer needs, its feasibility, and its potential for profitability.

3. Develop a prototype: Once you have an idea for a new product or service, develop a prototype to

test its viability. Gather feedback from customers and make any necessary refinements.

4. Test and refine: Test the product or service on a small scale before launching it on a larger scale. Use customer feedback to refine and improve upon the product or service before scaling it up.

5. Stay flexible: Be open to making changes and modifications to the product or service as needed. Stay agile and be willing to pivot if necessary.

6. Use design thinking: Design thinking is a problem-solving approach that focuses on empathy, experimentation, and iteration. Use design thinking principles to develop new products or services that meet customer needs and drive growth.

7. Collaborate with others: Collaborate with partners, vendors, and suppliers to develop new

products or services. This can bring fresh perspectives and expertise to the development process.

In conclusion, developing new products and services is essential for business growth and staying competitive. By identifying customer needs, brainstorming ideas, developing prototypes, testing, and refining, staying flexible, using design thinking, and collaborating with others, businesses can develop new products and services that meet customer needs and drive growth.

Creating a culture of innovation within your organization

Creating a culture of innovation within your organization is essential for driving growth and staying competitive. Here are some strategies for creating a culture of innovation:

1. Encourage idea-sharing: Create an environment where employees feel comfortable sharing their ideas and suggestions. Encourage brainstorming sessions and regularly ask for feedback and suggestions.

2. Embrace failure: Encourage employees to take risks and be willing to experiment. Embrace failure as an opportunity to learn and improve.

3. Provide resources: Provide employees with the necessary resources, including time, money, and tools, to pursue new ideas and innovations.

4. Foster collaboration: Encourage collaboration and teamwork across different departments and teams. This can bring fresh perspectives and expertise to the innovation process.

5. Celebrate successes: Celebrate successes and recognize employees who contribute to innovation

and growth. This can help foster a culture of innovation and motivate employees to continue pushing boundaries.

6. Develop innovation metrics: Develop metrics to measure the success of innovation initiatives. This can help track progress and identify areas for improvement.

7. Lead by example: Leaders should model innovative thinking and behavior. Encourage leaders to take risks and be open to new ideas.

8. Provide training and development: Provide training and development opportunities to help employees build skills and develop new ideas.

In conclusion, creating a culture of innovation within your organization is essential for driving growth and staying competitive. By encouraging idea-sharing, embracing failure, providing resources, fostering collaboration, celebrating successes, developing innovation metrics, leading by example, and providing training and development, businesses can create a culture of innovation that drives growth and success.

CHAPTER 3

Business Planning and Strategy

Developing a solid business plan

Developing a solid business plan is essential for starting a new business or growing an existing one. Here are some key steps to developing a business plan:

1. Conduct market research: Conduct research on your target market, competitors, and industry trends. Use this information to identify your target market, understand their needs, and assess the competition.

2. Define your business model: Define your business model, including your revenue streams, pricing strategy, and sales channels. This will help

you understand how your business will generate revenue and how you will reach customers.

3. Develop a marketing plan: Develop a marketing plan that outlines how you will reach and engage with your target audience. This should include strategies for advertising, promotions, public relations, and social media.

4. Outline your organizational structure: Outline your organizational structure, including key roles and responsibilities. This will help you identify any gaps in your team and plan for future hiring needs.

5. Develop a financial plan: Develop a financial plan that outlines your startup costs, projected revenue, and expenses. This should include a cash flow statement, balance sheet, and income statement.

6. Consider risks and challenges: Identify potential risks and challenges that your business may face, such as competition, regulatory issues, or economic downturns. Develop strategies for managing these risks and challenges.

7. Set goals and milestones: Set specific, measurable goals and milestones for your business. This will help you track progress and make adjustments as needed.

8. Get feedback: Share your business plan with trusted advisors, mentors, and potential investors. Get feedback on your plan and make any necessary revisions.

In conclusion, developing a solid business plan is essential for starting a new business or growing an existing one. By conducting market research, defining their business model, developing a marketing plan, outlining their organizational structure, developing a financial plan, considering risks and challenges, setting goals and milestones, and getting feedback, businesses can develop a plan that sets them up for success.

Strategic thinking and decision-making

Strategic thinking and decision-making are crucial skills for business leaders to have in order to successfully navigate complex challenges and achieve long-term success. Here are some key strategies for effective strategic thinking and decision-making:

1. Define the problem: Clearly define the problem or challenge you are facing. This will help you identify the root cause and develop effective solutions.

2. Gather data and insights: Gather data and insights from a variety of sources, including internal data, market research, and expert opinions.

This will help you make informed decisions and identify potential risks and opportunities.

3. Identify goals and objectives: Identify specific, measurable goals and objectives that align with your overall business strategy. This will help you focus your decision-making and prioritize actions that will drive growth and success.

4. Consider multiple options: Consider multiple options and alternatives before making a decision. This will help you identify the best course of action and avoid potential biases or blind spots.

5. Assess potential outcomes: Assess the potential outcomes of each option, including both short-term and long-term implications. This will help you make informed decisions that align with your overall business strategy.

6. Develop a plan: Develop a plan that outlines the steps you will take to achieve your goals and objectives. This should include timelines, resource allocation, and metrics for measuring success.

7. Monitor and adjust: Monitor your progress regularly and be willing to adjust your plan as needed. This will help you stay flexible and adapt to changing market conditions or new information.

In conclusion, strategic thinking and decision-making are critical skills for business leaders to have in order to achieve long-term success. By defining the problem, gathering data and insights, identifying goals and objectives, considering multiple options, assessing potential outcomes, developing a plan, and monitoring and adjusting as needed, leaders can make informed decisions that drive growth and success.

Analyzing the competition and market trends

Analyzing the competition and market trends is essential for businesses to stay competitive and succeed in today's dynamic business landscape. Here are some key strategies for effective analysis of the competition and market trends:

1. Identify your competitors: Identify your direct and indirect competitors in the market. This will help you understand their strengths, weaknesses, and competitive advantages.

2. Analyze their products and services: Analyze your competitors' products and services in detail, including their features, pricing, and marketing strategies. This will help you identify potential gaps in the market that your business can fill.

3. Assess their marketing and sales tactics: Assess your competitors' marketing and sales tactics, including their messaging, branding, and distribution channels. This will help you develop

effective marketing and sales strategies that differentiate your business from the competition.

4. Monitor industry trends: Monitor industry trends and changes in consumer behavior that may impact your business. This will help you stay ahead of the curve and adapt to changes in the market.

5. Gather customer feedback: Gather feedback from your customers and potential customers about their needs and preferences. This will help you develop products and services that meet their needs and preferences better than your competitors.

6. Use data analytics: Use data analytics tools to gather and analyze data about your competitors and market trends. This will help you make data-driven decisions and develop strategies that are based on insights rather than assumptions.

7. Develop a competitive strategy: Based on your analysis, develop a competitive strategy that differentiates your business from the competition. This should include tactics for marketing, sales, product development, and customer service.

In conclusion, analyzing the competition and market trends is essential for businesses to stay competitive and succeed in today's dynamic business landscape. By identifying your competitors, analyzing their products and services, assessing their marketing and sales tactics, monitoring industry trends, gathering customer feedback, using data analytics, and developing a competitive strategy, businesses can stay ahead of the curve.

CHAPTER 4

Marketing and Sales

Developing a marketing strategy that resonates with your target audience

Developing a marketing strategy that resonates with your target audience is essential for businesses to drive engagement, build brand loyalty, and ultimately drive sales. Here are some key strategies for developing a marketing strategy that resonates with your target audience:

1. Define your target audience: Clearly define your target audience based on their demographics, psychographics, and behaviors. This will help you understand their needs, preferences, and pain points.

2. Conduct market research: Conduct market research to gather insights into your target audience, their behavior, and the competition. This will help you identify gaps in the market that your business can fill and develop messaging that resonates with your target audience.

3. Develop a unique value proposition: Develop a unique value proposition that differentiates your business from the competition and addresses the needs and pain points of your target audience.

4. Choose the right channels: Choose the right marketing channels to reach your target audience, based on their preferences and behavior. This could include social media, email marketing, content marketing, paid advertising, or events.

5. Develop messaging that resonates: Develop messaging that resonates with your target audience,

based on their needs, preferences, and pain points. This messaging should be consistent across all channels and communicate the unique value proposition of your business.

6. Use visuals and storytelling: Use visuals and storytelling to create an emotional connection with your target audience and bring your messaging to life. This could include videos, infographics, or customer success stories.

7. Measure and optimize: Measure the performance of your marketing efforts and optimize your strategies based on data and insights. This will help you refine your messaging and targeting to better resonate with your target audience.

Building a brand that stands out in a crowded market

In a crowded market, building a brand that stands out is essential for businesses to differentiate themselves and attract customers. Here are some key strategies for building a brand that stands out in a crowded market:

1. Develop a unique value proposition: Develop a unique value proposition that differentiates your business from the competition and addresses the needs and pain points of your target audience.

2. Choose the right brand name and visual identity: Choose a brand name and visual identity that is memorable, easily recognizable, and reflects your unique value proposition. This could include a logo, color scheme, typography, and imagery.

3. Create consistent messaging: Develop consistent messaging that communicates your unique value proposition and resonates with your target audience. This messaging should be reflected across all marketing channels, including your website,

social media, advertising, and customer communications.

4. Focus on customer experience: Focus on delivering an exceptional customer experience that sets your brand apart from the competition. This could include personalized messaging, exceptional customer service, and a seamless online and offline experience.

5. Build a community: Build a community around your brand by creating engaging content, hosting events, and connecting with your customers on social media. This can help create brand loyalty and advocacy.

6. Leverage social proof: Leverage social proof by showcasing customer reviews, ratings, and testimonials. This can help build trust and credibility with potential customers.

7. Be authentic: Be authentic in your messaging and actions. This means staying true to your values and delivering on your promises to customers.

In conclusion, building a brand that stands out in a crowded market requires a unique value proposition, a memorable brand name and visual identity, consistent messaging, exceptional customer experience, community building, social proof, and authenticity. By implementing these strategies, businesses can effectively differentiate themselves in a crowded market and attract loyal customers.

Effective sales techniques and strategies

Effective sales techniques and strategies are crucial for businesses to generate revenue and drive growth. Here are some key strategies for developing effective sales techniques:

1. Understand your customers: Develop a deep understanding of your target audience, including their needs, pain points, and buying behavior. This will help you tailor your sales approach and messaging to their specific needs.

2. Build relationships: Build strong relationships with your customers by understanding their needs, providing personalized solutions, and delivering exceptional customer service.

3. Listen actively: Listen actively to your customers to understand their needs and concerns. This will help you tailor your solutions and messaging to meet their specific needs.

4. Provide value: Provide value to your customers by offering solutions that meet their needs and deliver tangible benefits. This will help you build trust and credibility with your customers.

5. Demonstrate expertise: Demonstrate your expertise by providing relevant information and insights to your customers. This will help establish your credibility and build trust with potential customers.

Use storytelling: Use storytelling to create an emotional connection with your customers and showcase the benefits of your solutions.

6. Handle objections: Anticipate objections and be prepared to address them effectively. This will help you overcome potential barriers to sales and build trust with your customers.

7. Follow up: Follow up with your customers to ensure their satisfaction and address any concerns or issues. This will help build long-term relationships and generate repeat business.

8. Leverage technology: Leverage technology to streamline your sales process and provide a more personalized experience for your customers. This could include using CRM software, marketing automation, or sales enablement tools.

In conclusion, effective sales techniques and strategies are essential for businesses to generate revenue and drive growth. By understanding your customers, building relationships, listening actively, providing value, demonstrating expertise, using storytelling, handling objections, following up, and leveraging technology, businesses can effectively sell their solutions and build long-term relationships with their customers.

CHAPTER 5

Financing and Funding

Understanding the different sources of funding

Understanding the different sources of funding is crucial for businesses looking to raise capital to finance their operations, expand their business, or launch new products and services. Here are some key sources of funding:

1. Bootstrapping: Bootstrapping refers to using personal savings, credit cards, or other personal assets to fund your business. While this approach

can be risky, it allows you to retain full control of your business and avoid taking on debt or giving up equity.

2. Friends and family: Friends and family can be a source of funding for your business, typically through personal loans or investments. While this approach can be less formal than traditional funding sources, it's important to establish clear terms and agreements to avoid damaging personal relationships.

3. Angel investors: Angel investors are wealthy individuals who provide funding to startups in exchange for equity in the company. They typically invest in the early stages of a business and provide mentorship and connections in addition to funding.

4. Venture capitalists: Venture capitalists are institutional investors who provide funding to

startups in exchange for equity in the company. They typically invest in the later stages of a business and provide significant amounts of funding, as well as connections and expertise.

5. Crowdfunding: Crowdfunding allows businesses to raise funds from a large number of individuals through online platforms. This approach can be an effective way to raise capital and generate buzz for your business, but it requires a compelling pitch and marketing strategy.

6. Bank loans: Bank loans are a traditional source of funding for businesses, offering fixed repayment terms and interest rates. However, they often require collateral and can be difficult to obtain for startups and small businesses.

7. Government grants: Government grants can provide funding to businesses for specific purposes, such as research and development or exporting.

While they can be competitive and have strict eligibility requirements, they offer a non-dilutive source of funding.

In conclusion, understanding the different sources of funding is essential for businesses to raise capital and finance their operations. Whether through bootstrapping, friends and family, angel investors, venture capitalists, crowdfunding, bank loans, or government grants, each source of funding has its own advantages and disadvantages, and businesses should carefully consider which option is best suited for their needs and goals.

Creating a financial plan and managing cash flow

Creating a financial plan and managing cash flow is critical for the success of any business. Here are some steps to help you create a financial plan and effectively manage your cash flow:

1. Define your financial goals: The first step in creating a financial plan is to define your financial goals. This may include increasing revenue, reducing costs, improving profitability, or expanding your business.

2. Forecast your income and expenses: Develop a forecast of your income and expenses for the upcoming year. This should include all sources of income, such as sales and investments, as well as all expenses, including overhead costs, salaries, and other operating expenses.

3. Analyze your cash flow: Analyze your cash flow by tracking your incoming and outgoing cash. This will help you understand your cash position and identify any potential shortfalls in cash flow.

4. Manage your expenses: To manage your cash flow effectively, you need to manage your expenses. Consider implementing cost-cutting measures or

finding ways to increase revenue to improve your cash flow.

5. Create a cash reserve: It's important to create a cash reserve to help manage unexpected expenses or dips in revenue. Aim to save at least three to six months' worth of expenses in a reserve fund.

6. Monitor and adjust your plan: Continuously monitor your financial plan and adjust it as necessary based on changes in your business or market conditions.

7. Seek professional advice: Consider seeking advice from a financial advisor or accountant to help you create and manage your financial plan.

In conclusion, creating a financial plan and managing cash flow are crucial for the success of any business. By defining your financial goals, forecasting your income and expenses, analyzing your cash flow, managing your expenses, creating a cash reserve, monitoring and adjusting your plan, and seeking professional advice, you can effectively manage your finances and achieve your business goals.

Pitching your business to investors and securing funding

Pitching your business to investors and securing funding can be a daunting task, but it is essential for the success of your business. Here are some steps to help you prepare for a successful pitch and secure funding:

1. Develop a compelling business plan: Before you can pitch your business to investors, you need to have a well-developed business plan that clearly outlines your products or services, market opportunity, competitive landscape, and financial projections.

2. Identify potential investors: Research potential investors who are interested in your industry and have a history of investing in startups. You can use online resources, such as AngelList or Crunchbase, to find potential investors.

3. Practice your pitch: Practice your pitch until it's second nature. You should be able to clearly and concisely communicate your business plan, market opportunity, and financial projections.

4. Create a pitch deck: Create a pitch deck that highlights the key points of your business plan. This should include an overview of your business, market opportunity, competitive landscape, and financial projections.

5. Secure a meeting with potential investors: Once you have identified potential investors, reach out to them to secure a meeting. You can do this through email or by attending networking events.

6. Follow up with potential investors: After your initial meeting, follow up with potential investors to answer any additional questions and provide more information about your business.

7. Negotiate terms and close the deal: If an investor is interested in investing in your business, you will need to negotiate terms and close the deal. This may involve equity or debt financing, and you will need to work with an attorney to ensure that the terms are favorable to your business.

In conclusion, pitching your business to investors and securing funding requires preparation, practice, and persistence. By developing a compelling business plan, identifying potential investors, practicing your pitch, creating a pitch deck, securing a meeting with potential investors, following up with potential investors, negotiating terms, and closing the deal, you can successfully secure the funding you need to take your business to the next level.

CHAPTER 6

Operations and Management

Building an effective team

Building an effective team is crucial to the success of any business. Here are some steps to help you build an effective team:

1. Hire the right people: When building a team, it's important to hire people who have the right skills and fit with your company's culture. Look for candidates who are not only qualified for the job but also share your company's values and goals.

2. Set clear expectations: Make sure your team knows what is expected of them. Set clear goals and deadlines, and communicate expectations clearly.

3. Encourage open communication: Encourage open communication within your team. This includes listening to feedback and ideas from team members and creating an environment where team members feel comfortable sharing their thoughts and concerns.

4. Foster a positive work environment: Creating a positive work environment is essential to building a strong team. Encourage collaboration, recognize and celebrate successes, and create opportunities for team members to socialize and build relationships.

5. Provide opportunities for growth: Provide your team with opportunities for growth and development. This can include training, mentoring, and opportunities to take on new projects or responsibilities.

6. Lead by example: As a leader, it's important to lead by example. Set a positive tone for the team, be transparent, and demonstrate the behaviors and values you want to see in your team.

7. Address conflicts promptly: Address conflicts and issues promptly to prevent them from escalating. This includes providing feedback and coaching to team members when needed and addressing conflicts directly and respectfully.

In conclusion, building an effective team takes time and effort. By hiring the right people, setting clear expectations, encouraging open communication, fostering a positive work environment, providing opportunities for growth, leading by example, and addressing conflicts promptly, you can build a strong and effective team that can help take your business to the next level.

Developing operational systems and processes

Developing operational systems and processes is an essential aspect of running a successful business. Here are some steps to help you develop effective operational systems and processes:

1. Identify key processes: Identify the key processes that are critical to the success of your business. This could include sales, customer service, production, inventory management, and more.

2. Map out the processes: Once you have identified the key processes, map them out step-by-step to gain a better understanding of how they work.

3. Identify areas for improvement: Identify areas where processes can be improved. This could include streamlining processes, reducing waste, and increasing efficiency.

4. Develop standard operating procedures (SOPs): Develop standard operating procedures (SOPs) for

each key process. SOPs provide clear instructions on how to perform tasks and help ensure consistency and quality.

5. Implement the processes: Implement the processes and SOPs and train employees on how to use them.

6. Test and refine: Monitor the processes and SOPs and refine them as needed. This could include making adjustments to improve efficiency, addressing bottlenecks, and incorporating feedback from employees and customers.

7. Automate where possible: Where possible, automate processes using technology. This can help increase efficiency and reduce errors.

8. Continuously improve: Continuously look for ways to improve operational systems and processes. This could include exploring new technologies,

seeking input from employees and customers, and staying up-to-date on industry best practices.

In conclusion, developing effective operational systems and processes is critical to the success of any business. By identifying key processes, mapping them out, identifying areas for improvement, developing SOPs, implementing the processes, monitoring, and refining, automating where possible, and continuously improving, you can create a more efficient and effective business that can better serve your customers and meet your goals.

Managing growth and scaling your business
Managing growth and scaling your business is a crucial stage in the life cycle of any successful organization. Here are some steps to help you effectively manage growth and scale your business:

1. Assess your current capacity: Before you start to scale your business, assess your current capacity. Determine if you have the resources, infrastructure, and processes in place to handle increased demand.

2. Develop a growth plan: Develop a growth plan that outlines your goals and objectives, as well as the steps required to achieve them. This plan should take into account factors such as market conditions, competition, customer needs, and resource availability.

3. Identify potential challenges: Identify potential challenges that may arise during the growth process, such as cash flow issues, increased competition, and employee retention.

4. Build a strong team: Build a strong team to support your growth efforts. This could include hiring new employees, training existing ones, and

developing a culture that promotes collaboration and innovation.

5. Establish systems and processes: Establish systems and processes to help manage growth and scale your business. This could include implementing new technology, refining operational processes, and automating certain tasks.

6. Manage cash flow: Managing cash flow is critical during the growth stage. Monitor cash flow closely, invest wisely, and be prepared to adjust your strategy as needed.

7. Maintain a focus on quality: As you scale your business, it's essential to maintain a focus on quality. Ensure that your products and services meet or exceed customer expectations.

8. Adapt and evolve: As your business grows, be prepared to adapt and evolve your strategy. Keep an

eye on market trends, customer needs, and emerging technologies, and adjust your approach accordingly.

In conclusion, managing growth and scaling your business is an exciting but challenging endeavor. By assessing your current capacity, developing a growth plan, identifying potential challenges, building a strong team, establishing systems and processes, managing cash flow, maintaining a focus on quality, and adapting and evolving your approach, you can successfully manage growth and take your business to the next level.

CHAPTER 7

Building a Culture of Success

Creating a culture that fosters creativity, innovation, and growth

Creating a culture that fosters creativity, innovation, and growth is key to building a successful and sustainable organization. Here are some steps to help you create a culture that supports these values:

1. Encourage idea generation: Encourage your employees to generate and share new ideas by creating a culture that values creativity and innovation. Provide opportunities for brainstorming and idea-sharing sessions.

2. Foster a learning environment: Create a culture that fosters learning and growth by investing in training and development opportunities for your employees. This will not only improve their skills but also boost their motivation and engagement.

3. Embrace diversity and inclusion: Embrace diversity and inclusion in your organization by creating a welcoming and inclusive environment where everyone feels valued and respected. This will help promote different perspectives and ideas, leading to more innovative solutions.

4. Celebrate successes: Celebrate successes and recognize the achievements of your employees to foster a culture of positivity and appreciation. This will also help motivate your team to continue innovating and taking risks.

5. Provide resources and support: Provide the necessary resources and support to help your employees innovate and grow. This could include access to technology, funding for new projects, and mentorship opportunities.

6. Foster collaboration: Encourage collaboration by creating opportunities for cross-functional teams to work together on projects. This will help break down silos and promote the exchange of ideas and knowledge.

7. Lead by example: Lead by example by demonstrating a willingness to take risks, learn from failure, and embrace new ideas. This will set the tone for your organization and help create a culture of innovation and growth.

In conclusion, creating a culture that fosters creativity, innovation, and growth requires a concerted effort from leadership and employees alike. By encouraging idea generation, fostering a learning environment, embracing diversity and inclusion, celebrating successes, providing resources and support, fostering collaboration, and leading by example, you can build a culture that supports these values and drives sustainable success for your organization.

Attracting and retaining top talent

Attracting and retaining top talent is a key priority for any successful organization. Here are some strategies to help you attract and retain the best employees:

1. Offer competitive compensation and benefits: Providing competitive salaries, bonuses, and benefits packages is an important way to attract and retain top talent. Research industry standards and ensure your offerings are competitive.

2. Create a positive work environment: A positive work environment can make a big difference in attracting and retaining top talent. This includes factors such as flexible work arrangements, a strong work-life balance, and a supportive culture that values employee well-being.

3. Provide opportunities for growth and development: Offering opportunities for growth and development is an important way to attract and retain top talent. This could include training programs, mentorship opportunities, and opportunities for career advancement.

4. Prioritize diversity and inclusion: Embracing diversity and inclusion is an important factor in attracting and retaining top talent. By creating a culture that values diversity, you can attract a wider pool of candidates and help retain employees who value inclusivity.

5. Use innovative recruiting strategies: Traditional recruiting methods may not be enough to attract top talent. Use innovative strategies such as social media recruiting, employee referral programs, and attending industry events to find the best candidates.

6. Focus on employer branding: A strong employer brand can help attract top talent. Focus on building a brand that highlights your company's values, culture, and mission.

7. Provide opportunities for work that matters: Top talent is often attracted to work that is meaningful and purpose-driven. Providing opportunities for employees to work on projects that have a positive impact on society can help attract and retain top talent.

In conclusion, attracting and retaining top talent requires a multifaceted approach that includes offering competitive compensation and benefits, creating a positive work environment, providing opportunities for growth and development, prioritizing diversity and inclusion, using innovative recruiting strategies, focusing on employer branding, and providing opportunities for work that matters. By implementing these strategies, you can attract and retain the best employees and build a successful and sustainable organization.

Developing a culture of learning and continuous improvement

Developing a culture of learning and continuous improvement is essential for any organization that wants to stay competitive and succeed in today's fast-paced business environment. Here are some strategies to help you develop a culture of learning and continuous improvement in your organization:

1. Encourage curiosity and experimentation: Encourage your employees to ask questions, experiment, and take risks. This will help them learn and grow and also lead to new ideas and innovations.

2. Provide ongoing training and development: Offer training and development opportunities to your employees on an ongoing basis. This could include workshops, online courses, mentoring, and coaching.

3. Foster collaboration and knowledge sharing: Encourage collaboration and knowledge sharing among your employees. This could include cross-functional teams, knowledge management systems, and regular team meetings.

4. Recognize and reward learning and improvement: Recognize and reward employees who demonstrate a commitment to learning and

continuous improvement. This could include promotions, bonuses, and other incentives.

5. Lead by example: Leaders should model a commitment to learning and continuous improvement. This includes being open to feedback, admitting mistakes, and actively seeking out opportunities to learn and grow.

6. Measure progress and celebrate successes: Measure your progress towards your learning and improvement goals and celebrate successes along the way. This will help keep your employees motivated and engaged in the process.

In conclusion, developing a culture of learning and continuous improvement is essential for any organization that wants to succeed in today's fast-paced business environment. By encouraging curiosity and experimentation, providing ongoing training and development, fostering collaboration and knowledge sharing, recognizing and rewarding learning and improvement, leading by example, measuring progress, and celebrating successes, you can create a culture of learning and continuous improvement in your organization. This will help you stay competitive, adapt to change, and achieve long-term success.

CHAPTER 8

The Future of Entrepreneurship

Emerging trends in entrepreneurship and business

Entrepreneurship and business are constantly evolving, with new trends emerging all the time. Here are some of the emerging trends in entrepreneurship and business:

1. Social entrepreneurship: Social entrepreneurship involves creating businesses that have a social or environmental mission at their core. These businesses aim to make a positive impact on society while also generating profit.

2. E-commerce: E-commerce has been growing rapidly in recent years, and this trend is expected to continue. More and more businesses are selling their products and services online, and consumers are increasingly turning to online shopping for convenience and accessibility.

3. Remote work: The COVID-19 pandemic has accelerated the trend towards remote work, with many businesses adopting flexible work arrangements to accommodate the needs of their employees. This trend is likely to continue, as many workers have discovered the benefits of remote work and are reluctant to return to the traditional office environment.

4. Artificial intelligence and automation: Artificial intelligence and automation are transforming the way businesses operate. These technologies can

help businesses increase efficiency, reduce costs, and improve decision-making.

5. Sustainability: Consumers are increasingly concerned about environmental issues, and businesses are responding by adopting sustainable practices. This includes reducing waste, using renewable energy, and sourcing materials ethically.

6. Virtual and augmented reality: Virtual and augmented reality technologies are being used to create immersive experiences for customers. Businesses are using these technologies to showcase products, provide training, and create engaging marketing campaigns.

7. Subscription-based models: Subscription-based models are becoming increasingly popular, as businesses look for ways to generate recurring revenue streams. This model allows businesses to

provide ongoing value to customers while also ensuring a predictable revenue stream.

In conclusion, these are just a few of the emerging trends in entrepreneurship and business. As technology and consumer preferences continue to evolve, it's important for entrepreneurs and business owners to stay up-to-date on the latest trends and adapt their strategies accordingly. By embracing these trends and staying agile, businesses can position themselves for long-term success.

Navigating the challenges of a rapidly changing market

In today's business world, markets are changing rapidly, driven by technological advancements, globalization, and changing consumer preferences. As a result, entrepreneurs and business owners face numerous challenges when navigating this dynamic and ever-changing environment. Here are some strategies for navigating the challenges of a rapidly changing market:

1. Embrace innovation: Innovation is critical for success in a rapidly changing market. Businesses need to constantly innovate and adapt their products, services, and processes to stay ahead of the competition. This means investing in research and development, experimenting with new ideas, and embracing new technologies.

2. Stay agile: Agility is essential in a rapidly changing market. Businesses need to be able to quickly respond to changes in the market, whether it's launching a new product, entering a new market, or pivoting their business model. This requires a flexible and adaptable organizational structure, with processes and systems that can be quickly adjusted as needed.

3. Focus on the customer: In a rapidly changing market, customer needs and preferences can change quickly. Businesses need to stay attuned to their customers and be responsive to their changing needs. This means collecting and analyzing customer feedback, monitoring market trends, and constantly refining the customer experience.

4. Build a strong team: A strong and capable team is essential for navigating the challenges of a rapidly changing market. Businesses need to recruit and retain top talent, with the skills and experience needed to drive innovation and adapt to changing market conditions.

5. Emphasize learning and continuous improvement: In a rapidly changing market, businesses need to be constantly learning and improving. This means investing in training and development programs for employees, experimenting with new approaches and ideas, and

constantly seeking feedback and insights from customers and stakeholders.

6. Plan for the long-term: In a rapidly changing market, it's easy to get caught up in short-term thinking and reactive decision-making. However, it's important to have a long-term strategic vision and plan that can guide decision-making and ensure the business stays focused on its goals and objectives.

In conclusion, navigating the challenges of a rapidly changing market is no easy feat. However, by embracing innovation, staying agile, focusing on the customer, building a strong team, emphasizing learning and continuous improvement, and planning for the long term, businesses can position themselves for success in a dynamic and ever-changing business landscape.

Opportunities and challenges for entrepreneurs in the digital age

The digital age has brought about a plethora of opportunities and challenges for entrepreneurs. On the one hand, it has opened up new markets, enabled businesses to reach customers all over the world, and facilitated the creation of new products and services. On the other hand, it has also created new challenges, such as increased competition, cybersecurity threats, and changing consumer behavior. Let's take a closer look at some of the opportunities and challenges for entrepreneurs in the digital age:

Opportunities:

1. Global reach: The digital age has made it possible for entrepreneurs to reach customers all over the world. E-commerce platforms, social media, and digital marketing have made it easier than ever to

connect with customers, regardless of their location.

2. Low barriers to entry: With the rise of cloud computing, mobile technology, and other digital tools, the cost of starting a business has decreased significantly. Entrepreneurs can launch a business with minimal investment, which means that there are more opportunities for startups and small businesses to succeed.

3. Access to data: The digital age has generated vast amounts of data that entrepreneurs can use to gain insights into consumer behavior, market trends, and other important metrics. This data can be used to create better products, target marketing campaigns, and make more informed business decisions.

4. Automation and efficiency: The digital age has brought about a range of tools and technologies

that can help businesses automate tasks and improve efficiency. This includes everything from chatbots and virtual assistants to automated inventory management systems and data analytics tools.

Challenges:

1. Cybersecurity threats: With the increased reliance on digital technology, cybersecurity threats have become a major concern for businesses. Entrepreneurs need to take steps to protect their businesses from cyber threats, including implementing security protocols, training employees, and staying up-to-date on the latest threats and vulnerabilities.

2. Increased competition: The digital age has also led to increased competition, as businesses of all sizes have access to the same tools and technologies. Entrepreneurs need to find ways to differentiate

themselves from their competitors and provide value to their customers.

3. Changing consumer behavior: The rise of digital technology has also changed consumer behavior, with more and more people shopping online and using mobile devices to access information and services. Entrepreneurs need to adapt to these changes and ensure that their business is optimized for the digital age.

4. Rapidly changing technology: The pace of technological change is accelerating, which means that entrepreneurs need to stay up-to-date on the latest tools and technologies. This requires ongoing learning and professional development, as well as a willingness to experiment with new ideas and approaches.

In conclusion, the digital age has created both opportunities and challenges for entrepreneurs. By staying ahead of the curve and adapting to the latest tools and technologies, entrepreneurs can position themselves for success in the digital age. However, they must also be prepared to navigate the challenges that come with this rapidly evolving landscape, from cybersecurity threats to changing consumer behavior.

CONCLUSION

Final thoughts on the power of entrepreneurship in business.

Entrepreneurship is a powerful force that drives innovation, growth, and progress in the business world. Through the development of new products, services, and technologies, entrepreneurs can create value, solve problems, and change the world for the better.

However, the path of entrepreneurship is not without its challenges. The journey can be long and difficult, and success is never guaranteed. The most successful entrepreneurs possess a unique combination of skills, mindset, and work ethic, and they are willing to take calculated risks, persevere through failures, and learn from their mistakes.

Despite the challenges, the benefits of entrepreneurship are numerous. Entrepreneurs have the opportunity to create their own destinies, pursue their passions, and make a meaningful impact in the world. They have the freedom to work on projects that excite and inspire them, and to build businesses that reflect their values and beliefs.

In the rapidly changing business landscape of today, entrepreneurship has become more important than ever before. The digital age has created new opportunities for innovation and disruption, and entrepreneurs who can navigate this landscape have the potential to create immense value and impact.

In conclusion, entrepreneurship is a powerful force that has the potential to transform the world of business and beyond. While the journey can be challenging, the rewards are well worth the effort for those who are willing to take the risk and embrace the entrepreneurial mindset.